EMORY UNITED METHODIST CHURCH

I LEARN ABOUT SHARING

K 94

BY HARRIET A. ROORBACH
illustrated by SARAH KUREK

nashville   ABINGDON PRESS   new york

EMORY UNITED METHODIST CHURCH

Copyright © 1968 by Abingdon Press. All Rights Reserved. Printed in the United States of America. Library of Congress Catalog Card Number: 68-10706

ISBN 0-687-18516-5

To my sister, Rosemary

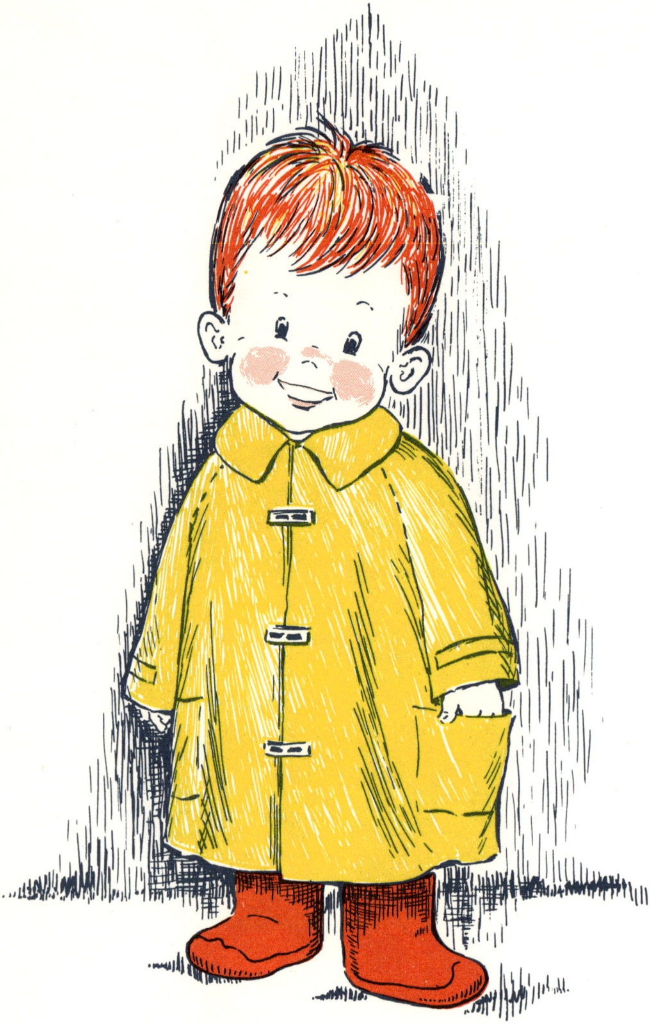

My name is Philip. Sometimes I am called "Phil," but my name is Philip. My father's name is Philip. He says he gave me that name. He says it is very nice to share a name with someone else.

"What is share?" I asked.

"To share means to give," said my father.

"Oh, like a present?"

"Yes, sometimes sharing is like a present, but there are many ways of sharing."

I am learning what it means to share. Susan is my baby sister. Sometimes when I am very busy playing, Mother asks me to take care of Susan. I don't always want to do this, but Mother says this is a way of sharing my time.

My friend Donna is sick and has to stay in bed. I am going to take her my bowl of goldfish to watch.

"That is a very good thing to do," said Mother. "It will keep Donna from being lonely while she has to stay inside.

"And Philip," added my mother, "letting Donna enjoy your goldfish is another way of sharing."

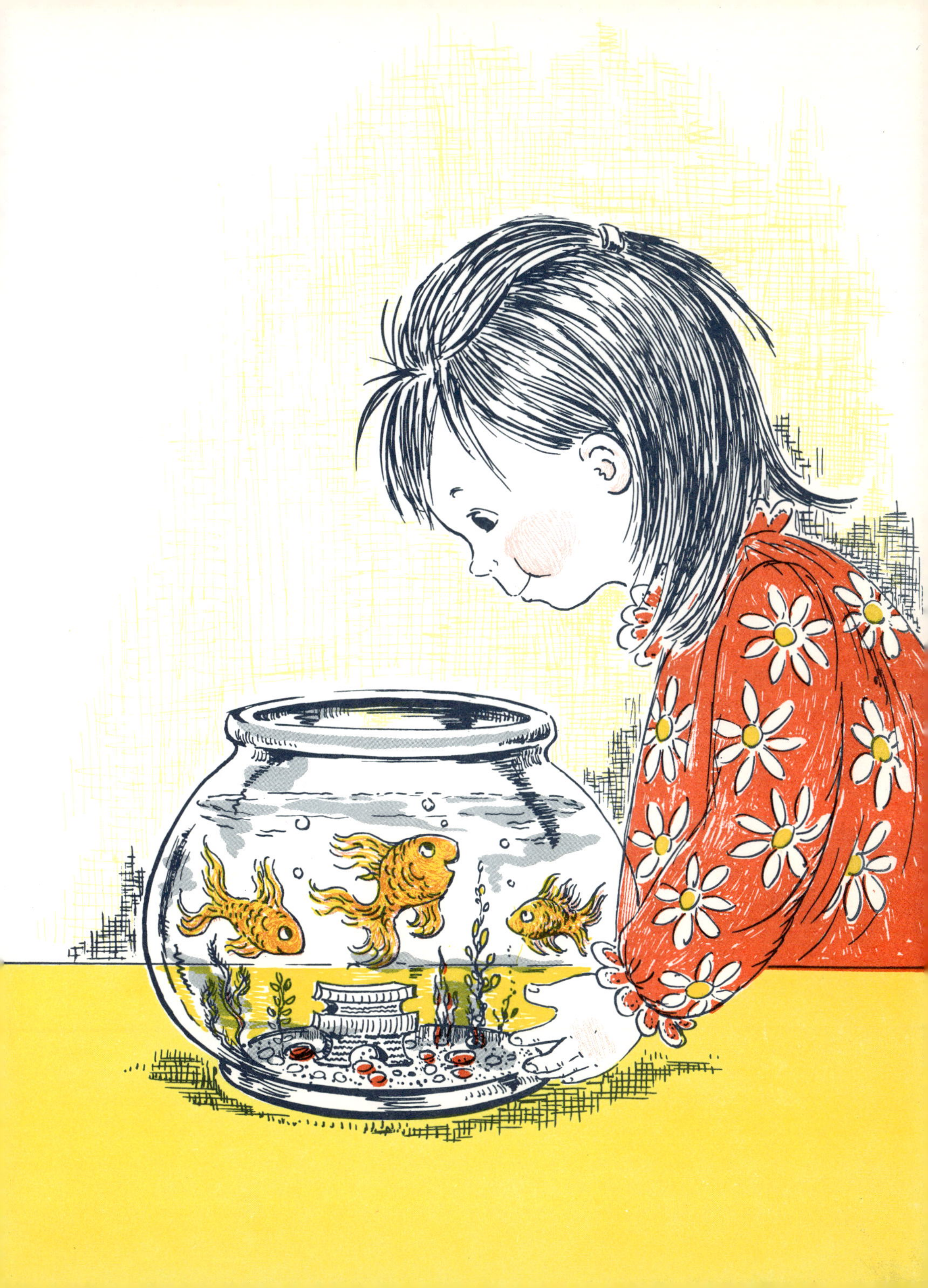

One day in our church school class, we were drawing a mural. Each one of us added a part to make a big picture. Martha drew the street and the trees. Jim drew a house. Brian made a church building with a steeple. Carol drew a car.

"I can only draw circles. What good are circles?" I asked.

"Circles look like clouds," answered Carol. "Philip, your circles can be the clouds in the sky."

"Everybody's work is important," Mrs. Stevens told us. "No one can do everything well. God wants us to share the things we can do with one another."

One day we looked at pictures of boys and girls in Halloween costumes. Each child was carrying a box with printed letters on it:

U N I C E F

Mrs. Stevens said the children in the pictures had collected money on Halloween to buy milk and medicine for boys and girls in other countries.

My brother Bill and I did that on Halloween. Bill was a ghost, and I was a goblin.

We went to lots of houses. After we had shouted, "Trick or treat!" we asked people to put money in the UNICEF box.

"Nearly everybody is sharing," said Bill.

At Christmastime, Mrs. Stevens asked us to bring a favorite toy or a book for the children at the community center.

"If you give something you like very much," she said, "it is a special kind of sharing."

"I like to play with all my toys and to look at the books," I said. "I don't think I want to give one of them away."

"How would you feel if you had no toys?" asked Mrs. Stevens. "Would you want some other boy to share with you?"

"Yes," I said, "yes, I would."

I put my favorite book in the box for the children at the community center. I knew some other boy or girl would like that book as much as I did. It was a special kind of sharing.

Mrs. Stevens placed her finger on the big world globe.

"Right here," she told us, "are children who are cold. I wonder if we can help fill the box of clothing that people are sending to help them be warm?"

"Mittens! Mittens! Let's all bring mittens," we suggested.

That is how a mitten tree bloomed in our room, so that other boys and girls far away could have warm hands.

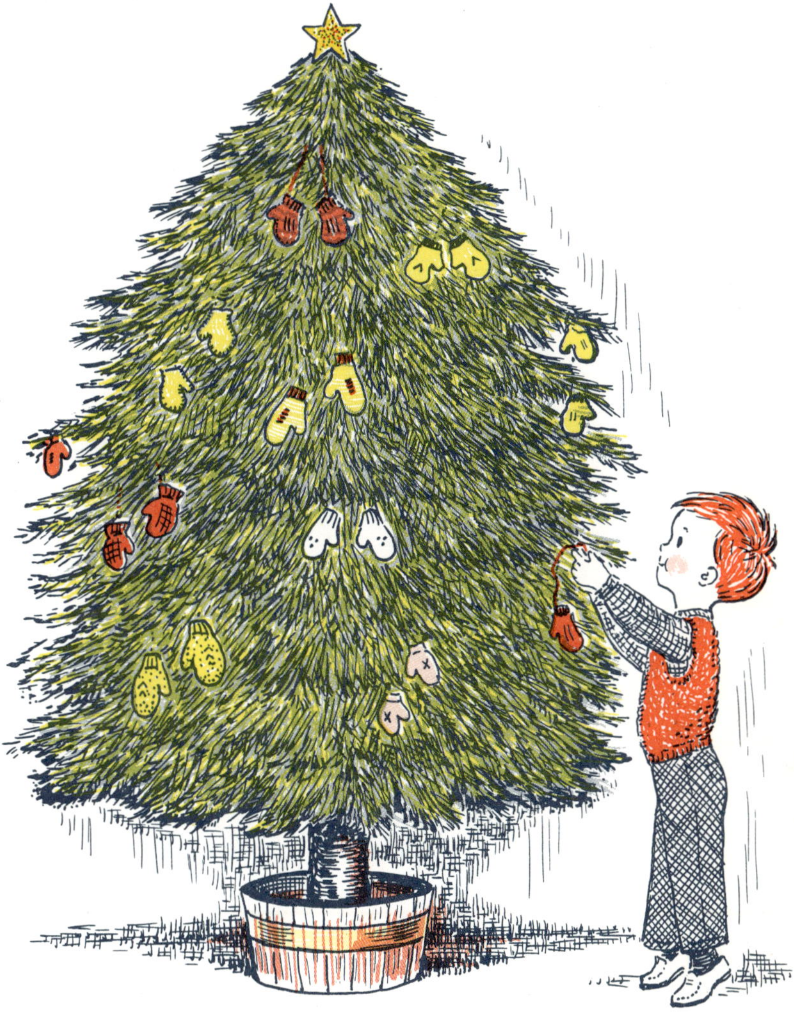

I looked out the window one morning, and the ground was covered with snow.

"Where will the birds get food?" I asked my mother.

"We will put bread crumbs out for them," she answered. "We will help take care of them. It is another way of sharing."

Mrs. Allen is our friend. We wanted her to know we loved her. Today we brought apples and grapes and oranges to our classroom. We packed the fruit in a basket and wrapped it with paper and pretty ribbon.

Some of us went with Mrs. Stevens to take the basket to Mrs. Allen.

As we walked along, Carol asked Mrs. Stevens, "Are we sharing with Mrs. Allen?"

"Yes," said Mrs. Stevens. "When you show someone you love her, that is a way of sharing."

When my father gave me my allowance, he said, "Philip, you must think about how you will use this. Money is needed for many things. You could spend your allowance every week on the things you want, but that isn't the best way. Save a part of it to share with others."

Thinking about how to spend my allowance is one way I am learning what it means to share.

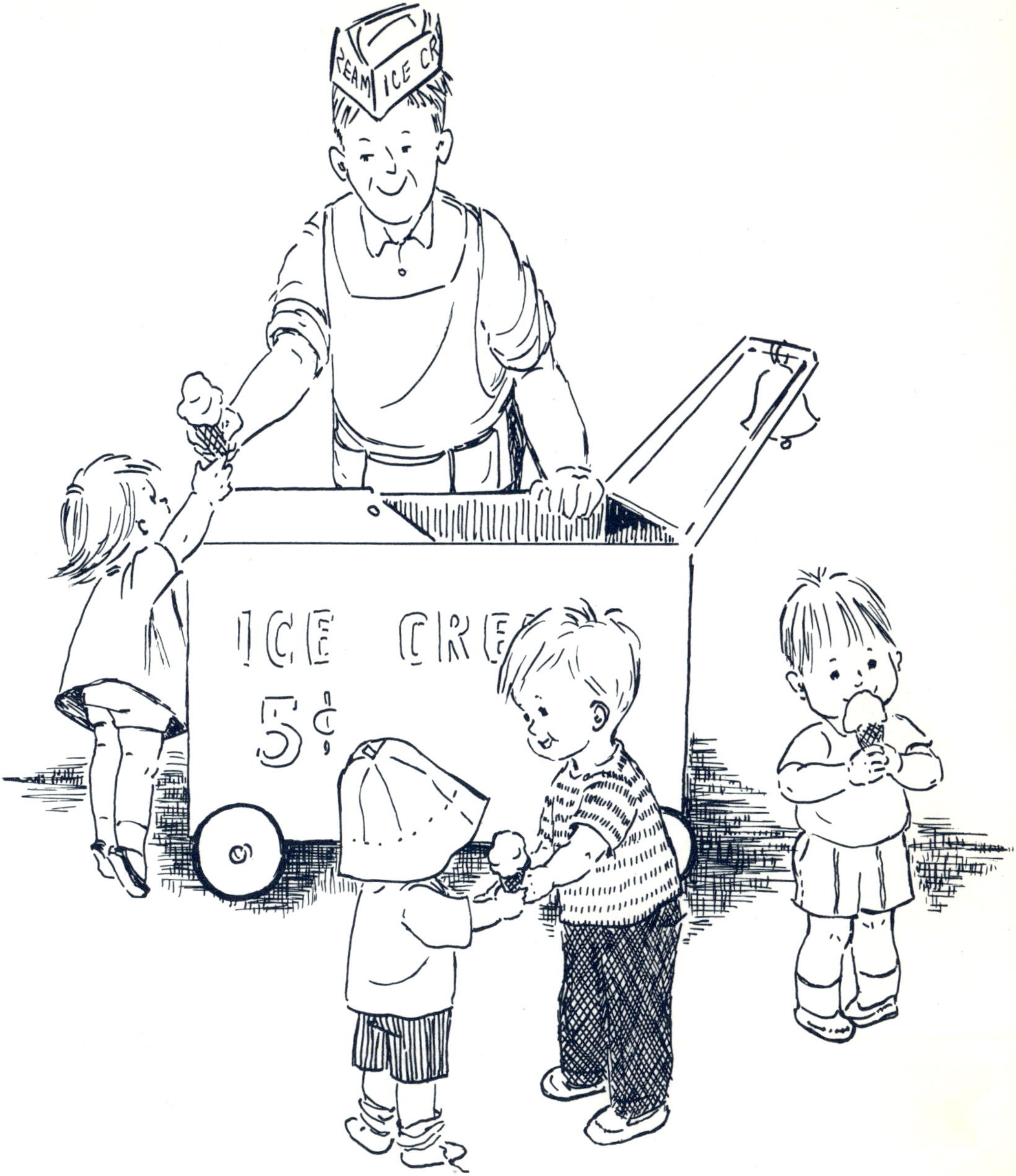

ICE CR
ICE CRE
5¢

I am learning that the offering money I take to church does many things. It helps buy books and Bibles and pictures and work materials. It helps build other churches. It helps pay all the people who work at our church every day.

Part of my offering helps pay our minister so he can preach, visit the sick, and talk with people who need his help.

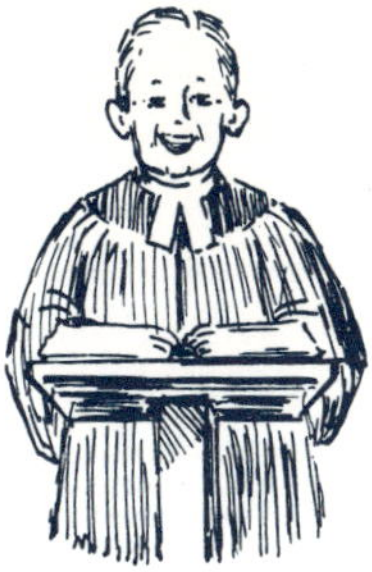

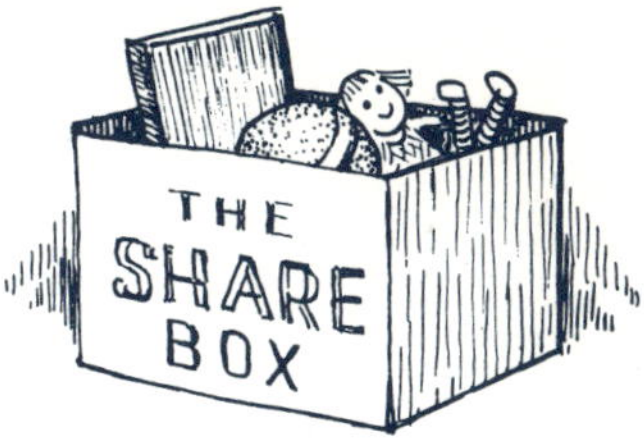
THE
SHARE
BOX

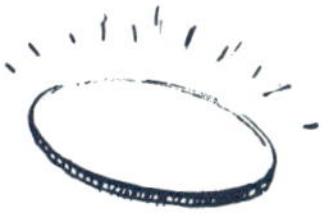

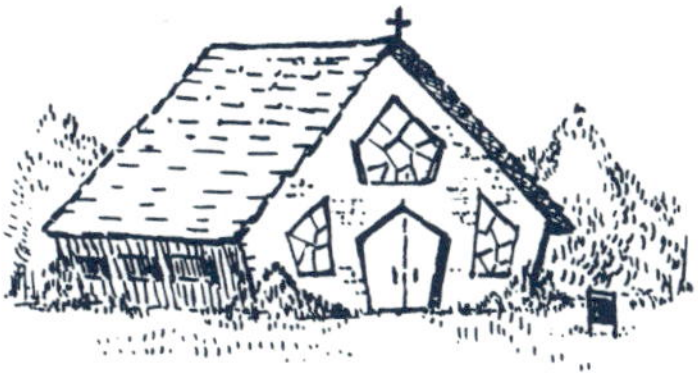

HOLY
BIBLE

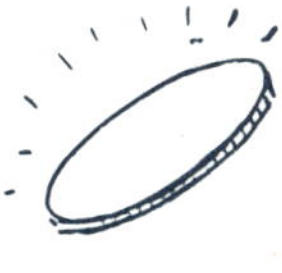

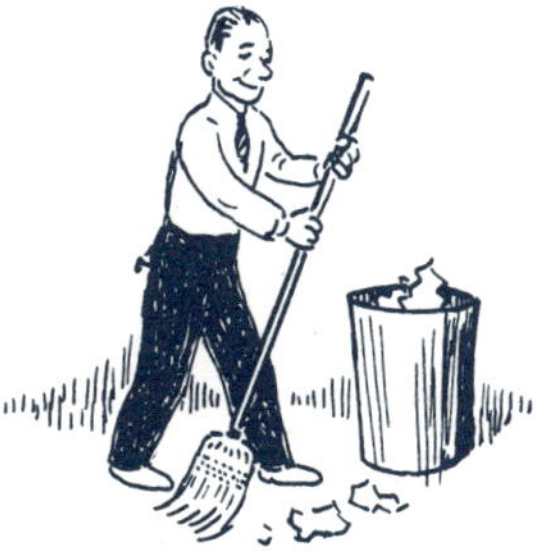

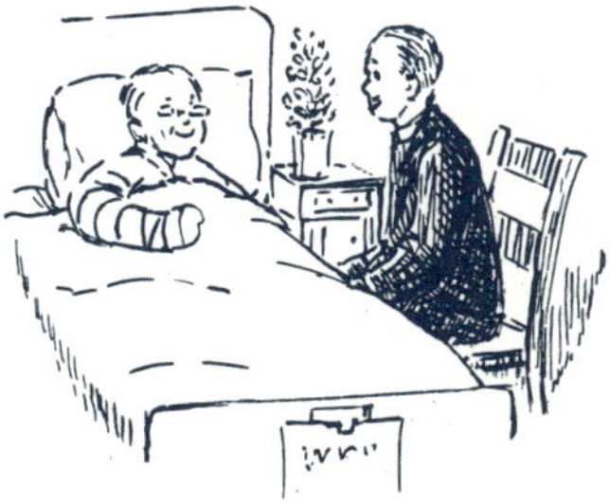

The offering we give helps pay **Mr. Howard**, who keeps our church building clean. I help him in other ways, too. When I remember to pick up the scraps from the floor on Sunday, I am sharing my time with Mr. Howard.

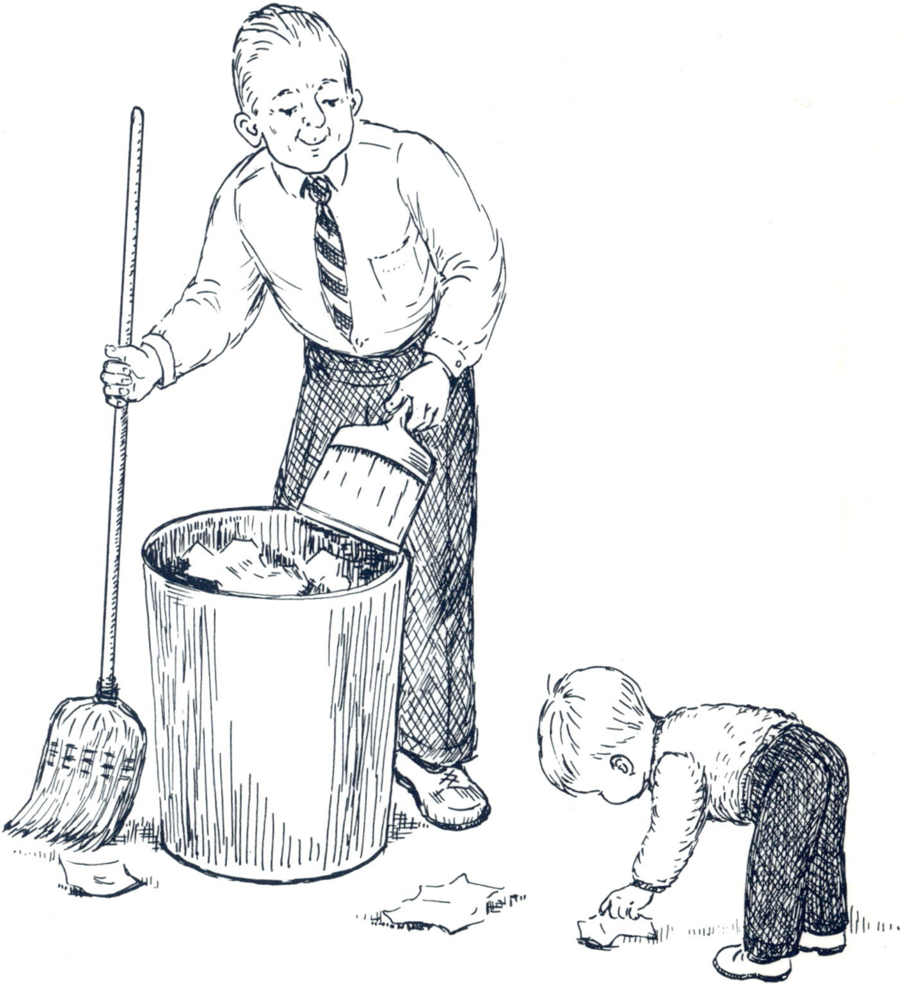

I am learning that part of my offering helps people in other countries.

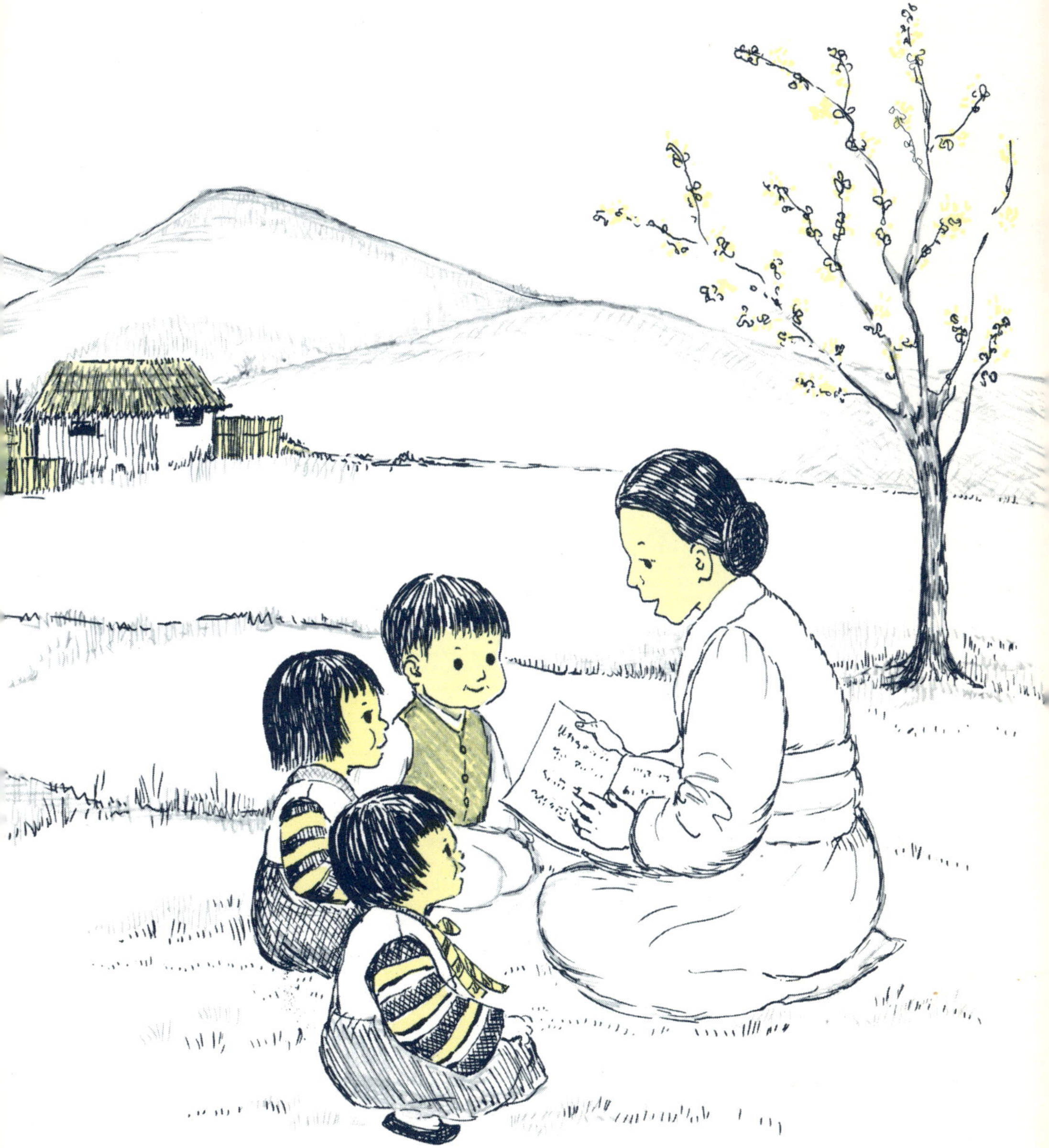

There are many ways to share. I am glad
I can share my time, my food, my toys, my

clothing, my money, and the things I can do,
to help others.

I am glad to share this book with *you*.

K94

Roorbach

I Learn About Sharing

DATE	ISSUED TO
MY 22	Kyn to 74 — Mustard
	Cati C.
SEP 24	Caruth
	Lauren Whitney

EMORY UNITED METHODIST CHURCH